"What was that?" he wondered,
and he set off to explore.

Danny soon found Tilly,
who was **stomping** round with glee.

"Did you go BOOM?" asked Danny.
But she said, "It wasn't me!"

STOMP!

Danny kept on walking
and saw Victor **whoosh** ahead.

WHOOOO

OSH!

"Did you go BOOM?" asked Danny.
But Victor shook his head.

Nearby, Dawn was **crunching** leaves,
and standing big and tall.

"Did you go BOOM?" asked Danny.
But Dawn said, "Not at all!"

CRUNCH!

Danny soon saw T. rex Tom,
the grumpy dinosaur.

"Did you go BOOM?" asked Danny.
But Tom just gave a ROARRR!

Danny Dino then looked up
at something big and red.

The volcano gave a noisy BOOM.
"That's it!" Danny said.

He turned to go, then heard a CRACK.
"What was that?" he said.